Handwritten list (left margin):
- GENTLE
- YEAR
- PERMIT
- RADAR
- PARTY
- STICH
- BEACH
- KITTEN
- BROOM
- NATURE
- OCTOBER
- SAIL

BeSWAT

Mike Hargraves

PRAISE FOR BESWAT

THE TOOLS TO SUCCEED AT LIFE

Mike Weir | PGA Masters Champion

"Being a professional athlete, I can appreciate and admire a disciplined approach to one's profession. In my opinion, Mike's professional career has provided him the tools to succeed at life. Mike's approach in BeSWAT gives one a realistic guideline to tackle head on the challenges we all face in life!"

BROUGHT A UNIQUE NEW OUTLOOK TO WHAT WE DO

Randy Gubler | Sr. Franchise Program Manager | Genentech

"BeSWAT was exactly what our sales team needed as we prepared for a new competitor. In the medical world, we tend to go through multiple workshops on an annual basis to become better leaders, communicators and sales people. Mike Hargraves was able to bring a unique new outlook to what we do and how we do it, past, present and future. As you go through Mike's programs, you quickly figure out it's not about teaching people how to become better leaders, communicators and sales people, it's about the preparation you put in, the people and resources you have access to, and the strategic plan you implement. The leadership, communication and leveraging of strengths seem to surface naturally when you do it right."

CAPTIVATED, MOTIVATED AND UTTERLY INSPIRED!

Christy O'Driscoll | Deloitte & Touche

"Mike left our company captivated, motivated and utterly inspired! Days later our employees were still talking about how he expanded the way they thought about things. He uses insightful clues into the mindset of how powerful organizations/groups cohesively accomplish their target and how that can be duplicated in anyone's everyday life. I'm very impressed! We will definitely be using Mike for further events as a tool for empowering our own people."

PRAISE FOR BESWAT

HE'S YOUR GUY!

Mark Maxfield | President/CEO | The Cottages

"I can count on one hand the number of people I have met in my life that I would trust my life to. Mike gets the number 1 spot. I don't say that lightly as he has proven that distinction many times. I would not hesitate to recommend Mike for whatever endeavor he puts his mind to. If you want a guy that has been there and done that, and excelled at all of it......he's your guy!"

A GAME CHANGER FOR ANY ORGANIZATION

Richard Eggett | CEO | Rockwell Time

"At Rockwell, we invest in our staff because they are family. BeSWAT Trainings takes this to a whole new level. It's fun and engaging, but most importantly the participants walk away with a warrior's mindset and a drive to be the best at what they do. The teamwork and leadership strategies are game changers for any organization, big or small. Mike is a highly effective trainer and uses his unique approach to bring out the very best in everyone. I strongly recommend BeSWAT Trainings to any organization looking to take their game to the next level."

THE REAL DEAL

Nathan Osmond

"Mike Hargraves is the real deal. There is nothing fake about him. As a speaker, businessman and former SWAT member, he has a well of knowledge and brings it to the table every time. I've learned a lot from Mike and view him as a mentor. I highly recommend him and his talents."

Copyright © 2015 Michael Hargraves

ISBN-13: 978-1533257666

All rights reserved.

BeSWAT™ and No-Fail Mindset™ are Trademarks of Michael Hargraves and cannot be used without permission.

Published in the United States

Chapter 1

THE CREATION OF BESWAT

Over the past twenty years, I have been involved with SWAT in several capacities; as an operator on a full-time team, as an instructor, and as a motivational keynote speaker. SWAT is in my blood and is one of the things I was meant to do. Unfortunately, most public servants like SWAT operators barely break out of the poverty level income bracket.

It didn't take me long to figure out that this line of work would not allow the type of living I wanted for my family, and because SWAT is more of a calling than a job, I had to find another way to supplement the meager living it provided.

That, my friends, is easier said than done! A qualifying side job would have had to be absolutely flexible allowing for me to drop everything and respond if called out. For some reason, employers seemed to take issue with that, so I decided that owning and operating my own business would be the best solution.

At first, my experience on the SWAT team was exactly the opposite to that of running my own business. **Never once, in over a decade of doing countless operations big and small did my SWAT team ever fail to achieve our objective.** We were faced with impossible situations and obstacles on a regular basis: fugitive man hunts, hostage rescue, prison riots, barricaded active shooters, gangs, and drug raids to name a few. Yet we always found a way to win.

My experience in business... Well, that was a different story!

I was a complete dichotomy. On one hand, I was struggling with business, frustrated and searching for success, yet on the other, undefeated with SWAT—sometimes *on the same day!* Naturally, I began to look at what was making my SWAT team so successful, wanting to find the disconnect between my two jobs and how I could bring the effectiveness of SWAT into my business life.

I dove in, pouring over every aspect of why and how SWAT did what we did, detailing how we executed our missions—planning, preparation… *everything!*

In studying SWAT, I realized that the missing component was the inherent mindset used by SWAT operators, the very same mindset that made the teams so successful and unstoppable. Once I embraced that realization, my mindset about business transformed.

Then, my mission transformed:

I set out to create an entrepreneurial SWAT team.

The SWAT mindset became the *No-Fail Mindset*, a strategy I could apply in business—*my business*—and to *everything*.

The power of a SWAT mindset works for athletics, relationships, and entire industries.

The strategies and topics in this book are not theory. They have been implemented on tactical teams to save lives, complete missions, and get the job done, time and again.

They work!

I know because my life depended on it. Not my paycheck, my job, or my reputation, but my life and the lives of others depended on what you are about to discover and implement in your own life and business.

At first glance, you may not think your life is at stake when you pull into your office and sit down at your desk, but it is—*your* life, *your family's* life, *your mortgage's* life—they're all at stake and that's only a glimpse into the strategies in this book and the ***No-Fail Mindset.***

Chapter 2

INTRODUCTION

With few exceptions, SWAT teams always win. In almost every circumstance and every situation, they win!

They have to.

SWAT teams do not have the luxury of making mistakes. A simple mistake can cost a member of that team his or her life, so the team must quickly identify the strengths of each operator and utilize those strengths in a surgical manner.

What's the recipe for success then? How does a SWAT team accomplish so much with such incredible precision in seconds? And how can you use the same technique in your business and life?

The No-Fail Mindset

The details are contained within this book, but in short the inherent SWAT mindset coupled with these ingredients, is the recipe for dominating all things in your world, whether it be business, or sports, or life:

Identify the strengths of competent individuals.

Link them in common purpose.

Arm them with special weapons and tactics.

Treat every situation like it's life or death.

Do that, and you're going to achieve whatever you want!

The content in this book is condensed and straight to the point by design. I want you to read it over and over! There are plenty of books out there that will give you your fix of war stories and complicated tactical missions. While those are interesting and fun to read, they're difficult to relate to everyday life. In BeSWAT, I not only expose the core of what makes these men and women so outstanding, but more importantly, inspire you to insert those details into your own life and win. This BeSWAT approach can be applied to your job, business, life goals, or anything—and I mean, anything—you desire. By applying the *No-Fail Mindset* and its strategies, you can take your life to the next level.

The stories within are real accounts of SWAT operations and experiences, pulled from not only my years on SWAT, but those of my teammates and other tactical operators.

The **BeSWAT Exercises** will give you a taste of the sophisticated exercises we lead in our trainings.

Chapter 3

THE NO-FAIL MINDSET

Motivation is the most discerning factor contributing to the success of tactical teams and that's also true for anyone with a goal, whether a businessman looking to motivate his employees, an employee shooting for advancement, or an athlete striving for a win.

I've traveled the world and it doesn't matter which group I'm speaking to, the number one answer when I ask the question of what motivates them is:

Money!

Considering the many other factors that drive the masses to go to work everyday there are obvious incentives for the worker, be it security, accolades, or the almighty dollar. And until something better comes along they choose to retain that job. But even a financially motivated employee will screw up from time to time and there are consequences depending on the severity, ranging from demotion or discipline—and if it was a big screw-up, a transfer or termination. Nothing that can't be fixed, right? Either with a new job or taking the feedback, buckling down, and giving that current job full effort.

Now lets look at the mindset of a SWAT operator. (Keep in mind, the average pay of an operator on a SWAT team is comparable to that of a grocery store clerk.) What is the consequence of screwing up on a SWAT team? Almost every time I ask this question I get the unanimous response of *death!* Now, as bad as that sounds, dying is not the worst consequence. The death of their partner or the victim is the ultimate price.

The worst thing imaginable would be explaining to my partner's loved ones that their son, daughter, dad, or mom is dead because I didn't execute my job correctly—because I screwed up.

That is some serious motivation to be surgical at your job.

As SWAT operators we know we're the last resort. When we step into an operation we must go in with a *No-Fail Mindset* because

There is no SWAT team to save the SWAT team!

When SWAT is called out, it means everything up to this point has gone to shit! The cards are stacked against us, we're out-numbered, out of our environment, and our actions are going to be scrutinized for months by the media and others. Mistakes are not an option. Failure is not an option. Without decisive victory, we are screwed!

This *No-Fail Mindset* is an inherent part of being a SWAT team operator. This instinctive mindset was the critical piece I was failing to bring into my business.

In law enforcement and the military we're not always getting the pick of the litter. Gifted, talented, and brilliant people tend to follow the money and become entrepreneurs, physicians, CEOs, attorneys, and professional athletes. The truth of it is, these gifted people are gifted in that they've discovered the most important element to the success of anything—and what I'm about to teach you—the *No-Fail Mindset*.

This inherent mindset is how tactical teams can take a handful of average people and achieve the high level of excellence and perfection that is expected and demanded of SWAT. The inherent life or death nature of being a SWAT operator, organically shifts that mindset and turns the ordinary into the extraordinary. We only had to show them how to recognize that mindset, have it at the ready day and night, and have the ability to flip it on anytime they choose.

And you can discover yours, too. Any single individual can have the same level of SWAT precision and perfection, no matter their job, business, or goals. All you need is to engage the *No-Fail Mindset*.

The combination of the SWAT team's danger and consequences, coupled with the lacking quality of incoming candidates was my light bulb moment that exposed me to the idea that we are all extraordinary when given the right tools and motivation. The *AHA* moment was purely accidental; I happened to have the right combination of lenses and be standing at the intersection of my struggling business and my SWAT success to see the piece that could transform my life.

In SWAT, life or death is your mindset; a *No-Fail Mindset* comes with the job. You either operate at the highest level or you die.

SWAT's unparalleled success comes down to that simple secret of mindset. Other professions have elements of danger, yet they don't operate at the same requirements of perfection. Driving a school bus full of kids, operating heavy equipment, flying a plane full of passengers, or running a company with hundreds of families relying on you can all have devastating—if not deadly—consequences!

Discovering the ability to trigger this level of motivation *will change everything.*

Shifting into this *No-Fail Mindset* is the key to unparalleled success.

You can learn tactics and techniques until your brain hurts, but if you won't—or can't—shift into that type of mindset, all you'll have is a bigger arsenal, whether your weapon is meetings or employees or offensive plays.

When you discover the way to replicate this type of mental approach in yourself and within your teams the results are unimaginable—A team of people coming to work everyday with the intent to do their jobs to perfection. Not only are these people surgical at their jobs, they are actively finding and creating ways to become better than they already are!

Sounds great, right?

Now all we have to do is create life-and-death situations every day.

Not so easy.

Without a serious motivator like death, it can be very difficult to attain that level of operation, let alone stay consistent at that level.

We all possess this ability to be extraordinary, but if so, then why isn't everyone using it?

Let's evaluate this untapped phenomenon in human behavior. It's an instinctive mindset that is already in all of us. The *No-Fail Mindset* isn't typically taught, it's discovered. When we're inserted into the proper environment, we will use this ability, without hesitation, *every time.*

Don't believe me?

Consider the last time you saw a friend discover a hornet on him and his instinctive response.

Now, you could ask that same individual to perform the same response in public without the assisted motivation from the hornet and almost all of them would decline. Everyone has different thresholds at which you choose to engage at that level.

Through my years of experience in training operators, athletes, and business people, I found that by immersing individuals in live, high-stress scenarios, there will come a point in which each participant will first instinctively discover their ability to engage in this mindset. Once the mindset is identified and embraced, the participants can and will engage simply by making the choice to do so.

Once you discover that little nugget, the world will drop its drawers for you.

This, my friends, is the *No-Fail Mindset*.

Motivation is instinctive. What's not instinctive is the ability to call on it at any time for any reason like a SWAT operator.

I don't know what that motivation trigger is for you personally, but once you find it, your results are almost guaranteed. Motivation triggers can be money, family, security, or pride.

But to really take your motivation to the next level, find a way to treat every situation like it's life or death. For almost everyone—whether it is your life or another—the ultimate sacrifice triggers a motivation that is unstoppable. However you achieve this mindset, whether it is inherently built into the situation or it's self-generated, flip that switch. I assure you, it's not always going to be reactive, it's certainly not going to be easy, so do what it takes to get your head right. Personally, I like using mnemonic tools such as a wristband, a coin or other object to remind me of where my mind gets to go when I need it to go there.

As an example, I wear a ring of my SWAT crest all the time. It's a reminder of my No-Fail Mindset. For me, seeing that ring instantly flips me into that mindset. After a workshop, I give my students a wristband as a reminder.

REAL WORLD SWAT

My personal discovery of the **No-Fail Mindset** came at the SWAT school in San Louis Obispo, California.

The moment you're accepted on the SWAT team as a *Potential Team Member* (PTM), you begin to hear the stories of SWAT School—the dreaded 10 days in California which transforms you from a PTM into a full-fledged member of the crest. This SWAT School was designed and run by current and former Operators from various Special Forces and SWAT Teams. Some of the toughest guys I knew came home with their tails tucked between their legs for different reasons, from injury, failure to meet standards, lack of discipline, or just plain giving up.

This camp wasn't so much about developing the skills of a SWAT member as it was about checking the gut of the PTM. Our team felt that if you can make it through this course and graduate, you're never going give up on any mission or task thrown at you while on SWAT duty. That is the essential quality to know before you accept someone on the team. The skills of a SWAT operator can be obtained in specialty schools once you are accepted on the team, but the heart of an operator is either there or it's not.

Preparation for this school began the moment you were hired into the Special Operations Unit. Life as a PTM was part of the preparation and a constant probing of competence. This, however; only led to a five-day local SWAT school designed to determine the readiness of the PTM for the SWAT school at the marine base in San Luis Obispo California. In this school, you get little to no sleep so you can be evaluated when depravation kicks in. You are given missions that can only be accomplished when you are working together as a team. The objective is to weed out all the individuals (non-team players) prior to spending tens of thousands of dollars on them in SWAT school. Our team had a reputation at the San Luis Obispo SWAT school for only sending top quality recruits and they took that accommodation very seriously.

I'll spare you most of the details of the prep SWAT school. In short, it was a condensed version of the real thing although the drill instructors and cadre were a bit more pleasant, only because they knew some of the PTMs would later become their family and team members at some point. Make no mistake; they were still ornery, mean SOBs. There are however, a few stories that can't go unshared.

Have you ever read about or listened to the experiences of a war veteran or Special Ops operator and wondered, how on earth can human beings expose themselves to such dangerous or harsh environments? The better question is, why would they? The human mind is very convincing once it's committed. It will drive its vessel to do unbelievably amazing things just as easily as it will convince it to do nothing at all. Once that mental switch is flipped and the mind is set on being or attaining something, it would literally take dying to keep you from achieving your mission.

Every so often, when an operator decides to hang up the boots, a new crop of PTMs are jockeying for that spot on the team. Each one of them in the early stages of discovering how and when to flip that mandatory mental switch. For some, this instinctive mindset takes some encouragement to engage, for others, even more encouragement to disengage.

I'm reminded of a drill we used to test potential team members on their dexterity and cognitive skills without the use of their vision and ability to breathe. The drill consisted of filling a 5-gallon bucket with water and placing a piece of fruit in the bucket that would sink to the bottom. Placed behind the bucket was an unassembled weapon system. The objective for the PTM was to assemble their weapon while their head was submerged in the water completely. Once the weapon was fully assembled and function checked for accuracy, the PTM was then to retrieve the piece of fruit at the bottom of the 5-gallon bucket to successfully complete the objective.

This particular PTM needed no encouragement to engage in this mindset. He proved efficient in the dexterity portion of this and was able to successfully assemble and function-check his weapon. His cognitive skills however, were overridden by his sheer drive to not fail or quit the final task of retrieving the piece of fruit at the bottom of the bucket. So much so, that at the time it did not occur to him that his shoulders were too wide for his head to reach the bottom of that bucket and retrieve the fruit in true bobbing style. For a solid twenty-plus seconds we could hardly contain ourselves as we watched this driven PTM thrashing and splashing in attempt to get his head to the bottom of that bucket and complete his mission. In the end, we had to physically remove him from the bucket to prevent him from drowning himself.

When this mindset kicks in, you believe there is nothing you can't do. When operators find themselves in harsh or dangerous situations, this mindset is exactly what is needed to keep going and survive. This PTM just needed to find his intensity dial and learn to control his head. He went on to become a disciplined operator, leader and trainer.

While I was in the preparatory training, our *herd,* as they called us, had screwed up a few times by dropping gear, being too noisy, or one of the many things we were incompetent at.

The first time we made a mistake, we were given a mascot to carry. This mascot was a huge pumpkin that weighed over 75 pounds. They instructed us to treat this pumpkin like a fallen teammate, take it everywhere we went, and care for it like we would a teammate. At one point, the cadre stole our pumpkin and when we got it back, we were informed that our pumpkin had been sexually mistreated while in captivity and had babies. We were then given smaller versions of the original pumpkin to carry.

Now, pumpkins are not very tactical by nature. In order to protect both the pumpkin and ourselves, we camouflaged it by building a backpack that would fit around it. Needless to say, the largest pumpkin became daunting and we took turns packing the beast wherever we went. At one point, we were tactically negotiating down a canyon where our only available route was to get in the river.

We then came to a point where the river turned into a slippery rockslide that emptied into a deep pond at the end of the slide. The only way to press on was to slide down the slippery rock and into this pond all while maintaining our 360-degree coverage and tactical formation.

Keep in mind that we are in Utah's Wasatch mountains in the end of October, so the water was just short of icing over. When we reached the slide, the pumpkin was strapped to PTM "Weave," a wiry, skinny but tough mutha that went on to be one of the best operators I've ever worked with.

We went down this slide two-by-two, desperately fighting to hold our positions, plunging into the icy pond below and then surfacing with our weapons at the ready in anticipation of an ambush. As quickly as possible, we exited the pond and held the security for the members still coming down the rockslide. Weave was holding rear security at the top and was the last to enter the pond. I remember hearing him hit the water but never surface. The pumpkin strapped to his back took him right to the bottom of the pond. Finally, he released himself from the backpack and surfaced gasping in that undeniable, Utah backcountry accent, the words that would become the brunt of many jokes over the next decade, "I lost my AR!" Knowing the ramifications of a PTM losing a weapon, it was obvious to the rest of us that we were getting back in the icy water and finding the rifle—*and the pumpkin!*

Once a PTM passed the prep SWAT school and was determined capable and ready to attend the SWAT school, the pressure was on. You got one shot and if you failed for any other reason than serious injury, you were fired from the team. What followed was the return of shame, which is not something anyone with a little bit of pride wants to go through.

We arrived at the gates to the complete chaos of guys in black berets screaming at the PTM-loaded vans trying to enter. I looked at the van ahead of us and they were literally pulling people out of the vans and dropping them in the front leaning rest position, while throwing gear everywhere. I thought to myself, *here we go.*

No sooner than our van came to a stop, we had cadre swarming us like a pack of hungry dogs. Our team was squared away for a bunch of PTMs, but it didn't matter. Everything we did was wrong.

We were in formation within seconds and there were at least one cadre to every two PTMs. At any given time, five out of the eight of us were getting verbally rocked. The guy next to me had some monster of a drill instructor screaming in his face and I could feel the spit of the man hitting the side of my face.

In the first sixty minutes of intake, we were up and down, doing pushup after pushup. I remember watching the PTMs around me writhing in pain and thinking to myself, I am so glad I trained my butt off for this!

Intake continued in our barracks where we were evaluated on our equipment preparation. There was equipment flying everywhere and PTMs chasing after it like it was precious material. I recall one of the PTMs in our unit failed to *dog-ear* one roll of electrical tape resulting in the roll flying across the room and into the eye of a PTM. When the PTM responded to the impact and broke our formation, we were back in the front leaning rest and doing pushups to failure.

Once intake was completed and they had us in full tac. kit standing in formation, we were informed that we were now beginning *day zero* of our training. In other words, this first day has been such a cluster so far that it would not count toward the training. Every detail of this camp was carefully designed to mess with your mind and body. A constant evaluation of your mental strength as well as your physical abilities.

I'm not sure we even slept the first three days. If we did, it was abruptly interrupted by blow horns and drill instructor's screaming while pulling you out of what little escape a nap could offer.

When your body and mind are deprived of sleep, funny things start to happen. This was an essential part of our training and I witnessed first hand the crazy things people do when they are lacking sleep.

In a real world operation, you must be able to control your mind and body when they begin to fail you. People rarely discover this type of mental control. When one's body gives out or is in immense pain, most people will stop what's causing the pain. In reality, you can go for so much longer if you learn how to control your head.

Everyone has a different point at which they meet this mental physical dilemma, and it was an essential objective that each and every PTM would come face to face with in this camp. I was about as prepared as you can be physically for this experience and for the first few days I relied heavily on my physical abilities to overcome the mental side of what was going on. I distinctly remember using the pain of other PTMs to motivate and energize myself to press on. I knew I was in better shape than many of them and would remind myself I was only dealing with a fraction of the discomfort they were, thereby receiving more confidence and stamina. In a program like this, you can only fly under the radar or hide behind physical abilities for so long.

The first time I came to this point, my ego drastically miscalculated my result.

We were negotiating the obstacle course in full tac. kit. It was a course that was very challenging even without an extra fifty pounds of gear strapped on. I noticed a portion of the course that was causing quite a bit of attention due to the failure of meeting the objective given. It was a rope hanging from a frame with a bell at the top. The objective was to begin with your butt on the ground, climb the rope using only your upper body, ring the bell, and descend slowly.

As I was negotiating the obstacles before the rope climb, I noticed that nobody was ringing the bell. Cadets were falling and sliding back down the rope only to be ridiculed by not meeting the objective. My ego kicked in and I said to myself, "I'm going to ring that bell." When I got to the obstacle I dug into the reserves, climbed the rope and rung the bell. I remember thinking to myself as I was descending, "Man, that's gonna impress some cadres."

As I descended close to the bottom, I saw black berets swarming to me, one of 'em saying, "It looks like we have a special individual here!"

These cadres were just looking for the guys who were sandbagging, relying on physical abilities to fly under the radar and prevent having to truly experience the real gut check. That is when the real pain for me began. I was pulled to the side of the obstacle and a series of pain-riddled exercises were thrown at me for what seemed like an hour.

I was pushed to the point of physical failure fairly quickly and then it became a mind game. They were doing everything they could to get me to give up. Several times during this process I believed there was no way for my body to do another task and I feared getting cut from the school due to injury or failure to complete the task.

I had one tool left to use effectively and that was my mindset. I began treating every task like someone's life depended on it. I refused to give up and I never stopped fighting to accomplish the task given. This was when I discovered a self-generated motivation that unlocked reserves I didn't even know existed. More importantly, it taught me to never quit until the goal is met. It's gonna get dirty, it'll hurt and can be very unpleasant, but that's when everyone else walks away and you win!

Eventually, the barrage subsided for the time and I was able to move on.

In a camp like this, everyone must go to that level. One of the honors of graduating from this academy was to receive your SWAT crest. I never thought I'd be so happy to have a two-prong *crest* pin held to my chest while my teammates punched it into my skin.

It was one of the most rewarding experiences of my life.

Most of the PTMs that began this journey were unwilling to dig that deep and never finished. Though they were completely capable of doing so, they chose comfort in the midst of chaos. In this SWAT school, that mindset is quickly washed out.

BESWAT EXERCISE

1. Think about your job.

2. Now think about a person who means more to you than anyone else. (If there are several who come to mind, pick one.)

3. Now pick one critical component of your job.

Hold those answers and we'll use a football player to set up this example.

Sam the football player has a girlfriend, Susie.

What if every time Sam took a snap, he knew there was a really good chance that if he didn't do his job perfectly, Susie would die?

Would he treat that snap differently?

Now think about your answers to the earlier questions. Really think about them, just for a moment.

If you knew going into your job that if you didn't attack that critical component with everything you have and win, your loved one in #2 might die. **Would that change the way you do your job?**

When I ask that question, people almost always say that it would change the way they prepared or executed their tasks.

So you're not alone. Most people don't treat jobs and positions like that every play because that's not a consequence. If you screw up a client presentation, no one dies.

That mindset only comes on when we get yelled at or when there's a chance that we might lose our jobs. Only then do the stakes rise to that level. But you DO have the choice to turn it on and flip into that mindset *every single time*—we just don't recognize that it's a necessary component—*or the missing component*—to our success.

Facing the threat of death organically separates SWAT from the average person. Having the ability to flip into that mindset at any time is key to moving from the ordinary into extraordinary.

Recognizing that you have the same ability to flip the switch in your day to day events without life or death circumstances creates your **No-Fail Mindset** and is what separates the champions from the participants.

Chapter 4

THE RULE OF PERCENTAGES

Proper Prior Planning Prevents Piss Poor Performance! The 7 P's.

You may have heard different versions and on a SWAT team they are drilled in until it's a reaction as common as blinking. Without preparation, I promise you, Mr. Murphy will be in attendance. For those of you who don't know who Mr. Murphy is, he's the guy that makes everything go in a direction you didn't plan for. It's his gift to seek out the areas that have been overlooked and expose them.

This is where the rule of percentages comes in to play.

99% Preparation 1% Execution

For many of the readers, this may sound extreme or even backward, but let me explain. As much as we want to think otherwise, nobody's perfect. On SWAT we still have the expectation of surgical results and near-perfection, even knowing that we're not perfect.

If you're operating with 99 parts of preparation to 1 part of execution, where are your mistakes most likely to happen? Exactly where you want them to happen, in your 99 parts of preparation. It's simply a matter of percentages.

On a SWAT team, this rule goes into effect the day you show up to get your gear and never stops. It can range from training scenarios, routine practice, to *what if* scenarios you constantly run in your head. Repetition and correction turn into surgical techniques and disciplined precise results. Your reaction to stimuli becomes exactly what you expect. But make no mistake; it takes a lot of time and repetition to become that proficient.

You can create those results in your life by using the rule of percentages and deploying the *No-Fail Mindset*.

REAL WORLD SWAT

When I was still a SWAT pup in my early years of the patch, the essential code of preparation and discipline of the SWAT team proved to save my ass!

The mechanics of a forced cell extraction are simple. You have a job to do, you do it perfect, and never let up until the goal has been met. Teams of five operators are to be used—never any less. We watched hours of videos to hammer the details and their principles home (and repercussions for a failed extraction). In other videos, we saw firsthand when failing to perform resulted in one of their team member's being stabbed or hit. When a team member got hurt, their entire team had to pull out, regroup, and start again. In other videos we would see the ramifications of a team going in with four people instead of five. In that scenario, they'd have one appendage not being covered or one guy handling two at a time. None of these scenarios are safe. We couldn't afford to perform at this level. We had to perform perfectly every time.

Each operator has a specific and equally important job. Four of the five operators are assigned to an appendage—arm or leg—and that appendage becomes your world! The fifth operator is the *shield*. This is the first operator through the door and the bridge that yields overwhelming violence of action. To the reader this may sound a bit harsh, but when you see the extent to which these subjects will go to stick a shank in your neck, it makes more sense.

The SWAT pager always goes off at the most inopportune times. On this given night, my sleep was interrupted to the familiar sound of three sharp beeps. I grabbed my go-bag and headed to the Ops center to brief for a forced cell extraction at the state prison. I was assigned to the position of shield (Short of very few exigent circumstances, you will hit the subject as hard as you possibly can in every situation regardless of size, age, threat or even gender. This position was typically reserved for operators that possessed more of a Mack truck type quality than I did. I was the point-man type, blessed with agility and quickness instead of sheer size.) But on that day, I was the best choice for the job.

During the briefing, moments before the entry, we were reminded of the consequences of failing to perform perfectly.

We didn't need much reminding since we knew the stakes and were witness to the failures of those before us.

As the shield guy, I couldn't let up! Every team member's life depended on it. As any red-blooded SWAT operator would be, I was fired up and ready to execute this job perfectly. In this situation, my subject was a larger man who had covered himself with his bed sheet and was holding a shank (homemade knife) in his hand. When we arrived, he was standing in a fighting stance, sheet over his head and mumbling something to the effect of, "If you open that door, I'll kill you all."

As usual, our system was executed down to the finest of details. The team was in position in front of the cell door and I could feel the intensity and pressure of my teammates behind me. The inmate was given the standard order. "Inmate John Doe, you have direct order to submit to a strip search and being hand cuffed, if you fail to comply with my order immediately, force will be used against you. What is your response?" To which he responded with a colorful display of adjectives. Needless to say, he failed to comply and I could feel the pressure on my back intensify immediately. The team leader yelled out, "Pop the door!"

At that moment, all I could think about was hitting this guy as hard as I possibly could. The force was immense, and once the door is popped there is no return. All chances for submitting or giving up have passed and there is no way to stop this freight train. Even if the subject chooses at that moment to turn around and curl up in the fetal position, the subject is getting hit and hit hard. My subject chose to stand his ground and fight. Once the door had been popped it seemed like my feet were only on the ground long enough to steer the sheer force behind me to the point of impact and at that time I remembered my training. I hit this guy as hard as I possibly could. At impact, I remember this guy getting blasted off his feet and driven the length of his cell only to come to an abrupt stop courtesy of the cinder block wall at the back of his cell. No sooner than I could push myself off of the subject, every appendage of his was locked with a body around it. At that point, I only needed to keep the shield in front of his face to prevent him from spitting on my teammates or other staff that would be in his range. Perfectly executed forced cell extraction.

As you can imagine, the subject had some mental issues and had proven in the past he was not only a danger to others, but also a danger to himself. At that time it was protocol to restrain a subject that had intentions of hurting himself to what we called the "four point chair". After the subject was restrained with handcuffs, leg irons and hooded, (yes, the fear of getting spit on was always there) we escorted the subject to a different cell in which we strapped him to the four-point chair. As part of our practice, we had the resident medical staff check his restraints to ensure they were not too tight as the inmate would be in the chair until it was determined he was not a threat to himself. At that point our job was complete. Another routine forced cell extraction in the books.

It was late and I wanted to get some sleep. It seemed I no sooner shut my eyes and the pager was going off again. This wasn't uncommon, as it seemed many callouts happened in clusters but when I looked for the code on the pager, it just read a telephone number— my captain's number. I called and was informed that the inmate we'd extracted only hours ago was dead. I was ordered to report to the Ops Center to be questioned by investigators immediately. Further I was not to discuss the matter with anyone, especially the other members of the team that participated in the extraction. As you can imagine, I was nervous, full of anxiety and unsure of what was to come. I began to replay the entire event over and over in my mind and even began to question my actions. Did I do something wrong? Did I hit him too hard? What is the video going to show? Am I going to lose my job—or worse—get charged for the death of this inmate?

When I arrived at the Ops Building, I was immediately told to report to the Admin Building where I would be questioned by State and County Investigators. I had no idea what to expect. I walked into the conference room where around the table were several investigators and administrators. I was the first of my team to be questioned. There was an open seat at the end of the table with a microphone facing the empty chair.

As I sat down, one of the investigators pressed record on the device placed in front of me and the questions began.

"Officer Hargraves, are you a member of the SWAT team that was called to extract the inmate last night?"

"I was."

"And what was your assignment on that team?"

"The Shield."

"Officer Hargraves, how hard did you hit the inmate that died this morning?"

Talk about a loaded question, but before I could even think of what to say, my conditioned training kicked in and I said, "I hit him as hard as I possibly could."

An investigator leaned over, turned off the recording device and said, "Officer, you should be very careful on how you answer our questions today." He then hit record and asked the question again. "Officer Hargraves, how hard did you hit the inmate that died this morning?"

I again replied that I hit him as hard as I possibly could.

After my response, I looked around the room and saw concerned expressions from the investigators and administrators. Their reaction made me second guess myself, but my training was clear and vast.

Several more questions were asked and once they were done, I was ordered not to discuss anything with anyone until after all the interviews were completed and I was dismissed. As I walked out of the room, one of my teammates was waiting to come in and I remember thinking, "Shit... the way that interview was conducted, the shield guy's gonna take the fall for this!"

Hours went by and I had painted all the worst-case scenarios in my head. Finally, we were all called into the war room in the Ops Center and debriefed. It was there that I discovered what discipline, preparation and teamwork was all about. Each of the other team members was asked the same question. Officer, if you had been assigned to the shield last night, how hard would you have hit the inmate that died this morning? Every one of my teammates replied the same as I had, "I would have hit him as hard as I possibly could."

Our training, discipline and teamwork in this situation proved to not only protect me, but also the integrity of the SWAT team. The fact is, I couldn't have said anything different. That was how I'd been trained, over and over. *Every* time was the same. We never wavered. We maintained 100% consistency.

Although, you don't have to **do each tactic** the same way every time.

You have to **know** each tactic 100%.

We will never know for sure what the motives of the interviewers were, but from my experience, something or someone needed to take the fall and provide a political explanation for what happened that day. Unfortunately for other professionals involved, reputations were hurt and jobs were lost. While watching the news and media report about the tragic death of an inmate who was restrained to the *"Devil's Chair"* I remember thinking, "Thank God for discipline and preparation." Without both I could very easily have been the fall guy and lost my job—for *doing* my job. Those who fail to plan better plan on failing!

Chapter 5

RULES OF AN OPERATOR

To be part of a great team, you must be a great team member. Adding **BeSWAT Tactics** will maximize results.

Be A Master of The Basics.

Just because you have a bag full of gear does not mean you should be using it. Start with a solid foundation and once you have that, you can build anything you want on it. Keep in mind, you did not get where you are by not knowing the basics. Continue to be a master of the basics.

Be A Subject Matter Expert.

Define and Refine your niche of expertise. This is what gives you job security and makes you relevant in your industry. Be so good that if the Supreme Court needed an expert opinion regarding your position in your line of work, they'd call you.
If it's not you, you're not working hard enough.

It's Only A Mistake The First Time.

Never make the same mistake twice. It's just lazy and unnecessary. Plus, it completely screws up the Rule of Percentages.

Aim Small, Miss Small.

We are not talking about goals here; we are talking about surgical results and how to direct your energy when you're working toward goals (of any size). This term was developed by snipers who, despite the elements around them, must be absolutely perfect in their shot placement. In their preparation, rather than aiming for the bull's-eye, they aim for the very center of the bull's-eye (aim small), keeping the focus point objective smaller than the target goal. Thereby creating a scenario that will keep them in the bull's-eye even if it lands off the mark.

Share Successful Strategies.

When you find what works, share it with your team now! Hoarding the secrets to your success because you want to get noticed or because something was your idea and you want the recognition is a direct route to make your whole team suffer. On SWAT you *want to* share with your teammate because they're the ones covering your six. Success is not about your ego; it's about achieving a goal. If you make it about yourself you will get your ass kicked by a team that doesn't.

Third-eye Principle.

An operator's eyes should always align with his primary weapon. If your gun is pointed one direction and your head in another, it takes two actions to complete a surgical shot, thereby taking away the essential component of speed. Think about your primary weapon, be it sports or business. Maybe it's your go-to strategy to get the job done. You want your tool going in the direction that your eyes (or attention) are going. Focus on the right things; make sure you're focused on your primary weapon.

How many moves does it take to complete and where can you streamline so you stay focused and aligned?

Improvise, Adapt, and Overcome.

You must be a thinking operator. Battle, whether it is in war or business, is an ever-changing, evolving riddle. Successful teams must have thinking operators and operational flexibility in order to overcome the competition. The best tactics are the ones that work right now! That may change from operation to operation, decade to decade depending on the stimulus around you. Sometimes the goal is a moving target and having the ability to resolve issues as they change in real time is the difference between success and failure.

REAL WORLD SWAT

There was a time when *no-knock* search warrants were the standard for SWAT teams and their use was commonplace in the world of SWAT. We loved no-knock warrants because they gave us the ultimate element of surprise against the bad guys we were trying to apprehend.

As the pendulum swung to the more liberal/non-aggressive side, it became more common for the judges to issue a knock-and-announce warrant. This took away one of the essential elements for an entry—

surprise. Now, before we could enter that same bad guy's house, we had to knock and announce ourselves. Unfortunately, the ultimate price was paid when a task force entered the residence of a drug dealer.

They knocked and announced themselves. When no one answered, they entered, having fulfilled the *knock and announce* portion of the warrant. What they'd actually done was tipped off the bad guy who prepared himself and waited until the agents were coming down the hallway. As they were bunched into that fatal funnel, he began to fire blindly, killing one agent and wounding another. They'd lost the elements of speed and surprise.

As SWAT teams, we had to take that unsuccessful tragedy and use it as a lesson and teachable moment to find a way to improvise and adapt to overcome the situation the courts had created for all teams, both SWAT and non-SWAT, by handcuffing our ability to rely on the element of surprise.

To overcome this new obstacle, it may be necessary for SWAT to breach all the doors and windows simultaneously, gaining back the element of surprise by attacking the entire house. Breaching every entry point in the house and having guns in every room prevents the bad guys from knowing where to focus their efforts.

BESWAT TACTIC

Modified L

In the spirit of improvising, sometimes a team needs to have tactics to overcome a deficiency and in that instance, a Modified L is used to maximize positioning due to lack of personnel. On a SWAT team, an operator will take up a position which gives them the most optimal viewpoint on a structure. For instance, if there were four corners to a building, the tactic would place two operators at opposite corners to be able to view all four sides of the building rather than using four people.

The tactic can be used in your own situation, too. Just because you don't think your team is big enough, there are still creative ways to get things done. In business, a similar scenario might be landing an account, knowing you need more personnel, but being unable to devote necessary resources to hire them.

What is your Modified L? Think back over a scenario that didn't go your way because of a situation where you were understaffed. What could you have done to cover those responsibilities? How could you have changed the scenario to create a modified L?

KISS—Keep It Simple, Stupid.

I think I speak for most operators when I say this: I hate it when things are unorganized and despise making things more complicated than they need to be. If you talk to any operator about their gear, I assure you they know where every piece is, that it's securely fastened, and they know how to get to it quick. Whether it's your gear or your mind, there is no room for disarray. I look at the acronym K.I.S.S. as a mandatory component of your planning. If your plans are too complicated, your operation is probably too complicated, leaving room for error, mistakes, and death. Now, I'm not saying oversimplify things. Remember, it's only a good plan if it works

Hard Angles.

The angle to the immediate right, left, up, or down of the entry team. These angles present the most threat to operators and must be covered as quickly as possible. Effective operators will cover all hard angles almost immediately. There is a tendency to focus on what you can see, and/or what's directly in front of you. Worse yet, once your focus is taken, there is a stronger tendency to get tunnel vision and disregard everything else in the room. The hard angles are the positions that will get the drop on you if they are not addressed. You alone can not cover all the hard angles, so it's critical to use and trust your team in situations like this.

REAL WORLD SWAT

To a new operator, adrenaline is as common as sweat, and I assure you sweat is all too common on SWAT. Adrenaline can be your best friend once you learn how to control it. Problem is, its not that easy to control. Try sprinting up the side of a mountain and then at the top taking a timed surgical shot with your service pistol at a hostage taker from fifteen yards. Your heart rate changes the dynamics of the situation and the capability of your skills, unless you can control it.

Days after returning from SWAT school, I received a callout to conduct a *no-knock* raid on a hotel room full of gang members. Our scouts reported over a dozen bodies in a twenty by twenty foot room. I was fired up!

This was my first legitimate operation where I was in the entry stick.

As a PTM (Potential Team Member), the only action you really see is from the perimeters. This can be fun and exciting but nowhere near the adrenaline rush you get when the door is blasted and you enter into the bad guys world. Before an operator gets the honor of being one of the first to lay his life on the line and enter a hostile environment, he or she must first complete all facets of the training.

Still wet behind the ears from SWAT school, I was assigned to the position of backup man to the point, the second operator through the door. We knew there was lots of bodies in this room, and with only two points of breach, the door and window located right next to each other, it made things more difficult. It gave us even more urgency to saturate this room with weapons and violence of action.

As we moved tactically into position being careful not to give ourselves away, I remember my heart was pounding in the anticipation of the next few seconds. I had little to no voice due to the previous weeks of training and I was about to enter into an extremely hostile room of gang members who had a history of shooting it out with law enforcement.

As the breacher negotiated the opening of the door, I moved into a room so packed with bodies you had to knock people down to penetrate deep into the room. This wake of people were covered and controlled by the operators behind me and I knew I had nothing to worry about. My six was covered.

As I mowed through bodies well into the room, my field of vision narrowed onto a guy who would not comply with the orders being given. In a microsecond, he became the only guy I saw in the room. He was sitting down with his hands tucked to the side of his legs. Despite the orders for him to show us his empty hands, he would not comply. As I reached him, I yelled for cover, lowered my weapon to the side sling position, and went hands on with this subject.

My backup man came over the top and covered me as I ripped this guy out of his chair and planted him face first into the ground. As I restrained him, I noticed no resistance. It was then that my vision began to expand and I saw the wheelchair I'd just ripped him out of.

As you can imagine, the jokes went on for months after that. A day or so after the operation, my captain called me in his office, asked me to take a seat, and told me a story. He said, "Hargraves, have you ever heard the story of the old bull and the young bull?"

I replied, "No, sir."

After reciting the story which emphasized my lack of patience and narrow field of vision, he said, "Hargraves, do you understand where I'm coming from on this?" Dutifully chastised and feeling the story in my guts, I replied, "Yes, sir. I do."

He said, "Good. Dismissed."

BESWAT TACTIC

This is an example of a hard angles scenario I run in my advanced workshops:

I take five people from the larger group and lead them outside the training room where I can give them a briefing, explaining the scenario and how I want them to handle it based on the following:

You're now a SWAT team.

There are multiple bad guys—could be two, might be as many as six. They've taken hostages.

Bad guys will be identified by their orange reflective vests. Everyone not wearing an orange vest is an unknown bystander or hostage.

I leave them in the hallway with instructions to stay until I call them into the room. Back in the room, I pick bad guys, give them their vests and place all but one in the hard angles of the room. I put the final bad guy in the center of the room with a hostage, and holding a gun to the hostage's head.

The rest of the participants in the room observe on the sidelines as hostages.

I call the team in and without fail, when they come through the door, they focus on the one bad guy with the gun to the hostage's head and walk past the bad guys who were placed at hard angles in the attempt to take out that one guy they're focused on.

Then we debrief. I ask all the participants what went right and what went wrong. I ask if the team if they felt like they were prepared—most always answered with a *No.* Then I ask if I gave them training if they'd like to do it again, which they usually do.

Then I proceed to take them out and train them on lining up as a SWAT team of five until they understand their roles and we run the scenario again.

After that second run we debrief again, and this time we tailor the situation to their own personal scenarios and how we get distracted on points in front of us but miss everything in our peripherals that are in the hard angles. We talk through identifying those hard angles and what training is necessary to follow the rules of an operator.

Chapter 6

PREPARATION

SMEAC is an acronym we use to organize the process of planning, ensure all angles are covered and nothing is missed. We use a lot of acronyms in SWAT, but we're not the only ones; several industries use them, including the medical field. Acronyms help us to remember what's important, they help us to remember all the pieces of a structure, or a process because if we're forgetting letters, we're forgetting steps.

You know those obsessive compulsive types of people who have a place for everything, a schedule for everyone, and an action list to make sure it's done just right? As operators, we must think ahead and stay organized to that level of obsessive. Everything we do has to happen a certain way, with certain steps. It's imperative that things operate as we expect, or we're back to the ultimate penalty of death—for us or a team member.

As with everything we've addressed to this point, there is a way to be organized that fits your company, team, or organization's goals and objectives. There's no right or wrong way to be organized, what's important is that you've scrutinized every single detail and individual to the level we've addressed as a **BeSWAT** level. A **BeSWAT** organization enables each member to focus on what they do best.

SMEAC—Situation. Mission. Execution. Administration & Logistics. Control & Communications.

Situation.

A brief description of the status of things right now, things like where you are, who is with you, the weather, or obstacles you must navigate through. These are considerations that may affect what you have to do.

Mission.

What needs to be accomplished.

Execution.

The rule of percentages tells us that by the time we execute we should have 99 additional parts of preparation. Part of this preparation is having plans in place when it's time to execute. These are the nuts and bolts detailed plans on how the unit will accomplish their mission. As you have probably guessed by now, one plan wont do. For every objective we want to have at least three plans in place. We call this PCG. Yes, it's an acronym within an acronym, but that's how we roll on SWAT.

P—The Primary Plan

This will typically be the best plan of action. This plan is designed and used for deliberate action and has considered all known factors. This plan is created to deliver surgical results and is custom tailored to each specific situation.

Sometimes things don't go as planned and if there's a malfunction with your weapon (presentation, offensive play) you don't have time to fix the malfunction because

you're in the heat of things. For SWAT, this might mean transitioning to a secondary weapon, or a secondary plan, but we always know our contingency plans before we ever set foot on the scenario so we can immediately put it in play when needed.

C—The Contingency Plan

This is your backup plan due to unforeseen issues like Mr. Murphy showing up. Though these angles are unlikely if your primary plan is thorough, they are best identified by running *what if* scenarios with the unit and working through solutions as they come up.

G—The Go-to-hell Plan

Because there is no SWAT team to save the SWAT team, this is the backup to the backup. This is where you pull out all the stops and win at all costs. What may be suppressive fire for a SWAT team, could be a company's bottom-line bid, or offering something to the client that the competition won't. At this point, you have to know what you're willing to do to come out on top and be ok with the wake you leave to get there. For a SWAT team it's fairly cut and dry. We are there to save lives and if that means giving our lives to save the innocent, we have come to terms with that long before we find ourselves in the situation. In business this could be a pre-designated point in the profit margin to where it becomes either worth it or not for the company. Whatever it is, this plan should be in place before it's needed so that it can be implemented at any time. The go-to-hell plan can also be used as a plan to provide overwhelming presence at a moment's notice. In SWAT we call this immediate action, and it's used when there is no time to construct a deliberate plan of action.

Now, back to SMEAC for the last two segments.

Administration & Logistics:

This addresses the support that is needed to accomplish the mission. Things like equipment, support, food, transportation, or additional personnel.

Control & Communications:

Complete control of perimeter and operation as well as proper communication with media and administration. This provides the relay of communication between administration, perimeter, and operations to ensure everyone is working together. It also provides information regarding transitions such as a break in the chain of command or shifting to a different plan.

Now like I said, there is no right or wrong in how you create organization within your operation. The important thing is that you are organized to the extreme, that you have 99 parts of preparation to 1 part of execution. Organization at that level is critical because it enables you to think ahead, focus on specialties, and improvise, adapt, and overcome if the need presents itself.
 This level of preparation takes a lot of time.
 The actor, Will Smith has a great quote about perseverance that I want to use to illustrate the importance of preparing to this **BeSWAT** level. He said:

"The only thing that I see that is distinctly different about me is I'm not afraid to die on a treadmill. I will not be out-worked, period. You might have more talent than me, you might be smarter than me, you might be sexier than me, you might be all of those things and you've got it on me in nine categories. But if we get on the treadmill together, there's two things: You're getting off first, or I'm going to die. It's really that simple, right? You're not going to out-work me. It's such a simple, basic concept. The guy who is willing to hustle the most is going to be the guy that just gets that loose ball. The majority of people who aren't getting the places they want or aren't achieving the things that they want in this business is strictly based on hustle. It's strictly based on being out-worked; it's strictly based on missing crucial opportunities. I say all the time if you stay ready, you ain't gotta get ready."

If you stay ready, you never have to cram, If you're cramming, you're going to die.

If you've done your homework, if you've put in the time and the hours and the consistency, you become unbeatable. Period. Yes, it's hard work.

How bad do you want it?

BESWAT EXERCISE

Think about the non-negotiable processes and procedures in your business.

Think about a time when you've missed a step and it's cost you a goal, or a client, or put something at risk. How can you put the steps in an order and create an unforgettable acronym? Who on your team needs to start using the acronym immediately? How can you use these acronyms in day-to-day activities?

Chapter 7

REMOVE THE DRAMA

When executing a mission, its time to flip the switch. How many times have you seen professionals become amateurs because of something that is happening behind the scenes? Each of us has personal biases, conflicts, or issues we are dealing with at any given moment. You're a professional and the best at what you do, so having a bad day or arguing with the spouse is not an excuse to be anything less than surgical.

REAL WORLD SWAT

We all have our buttons; one of mine is the neglect and abuse of children. Or, for that matter, anyone who is unable or unfit to protect themselves from predators. The Team was called out to do a *no-knock* raid on a known drug house in a rough part of town. I kicked the last interior door at the end of the hallway to find a couple under the influence of drugs and doing the *wild thing* on the bed. Upon seeing a barrage of balaclavas and barrels, they assumed the fetal position.

The drugs were in plain sight, the room was so cluttered we could barely clear it and the smell was downright disturbing. It's a common sight in residences where the occupants care more about drugs than themselves or their surroundings. That's not what bothered me. While clearing the back of the room and sifting through the piles of dirty clothes and junk, I saw a stroller in the corner. It was dirty and I could see something inside. My immediate thought was it must be a baby doll in there. Nope, the baby was real. I was surprised to see that the baby was not crying even after all the commotion.

I finished clearing the room and secured the baby and called for someone to extract the infant to the strong hold. Once the child was removed, I became enraged. This is one of those times when I was grateful for a partner who had my six and keeping his head clear and focused. He physically stood in front of me to keep the subjects at a safe distance while I unleashed a verbal lashing to a pair of half-baked morons. Then, he quietly reminded me of the job at hand and snapped me out of it.

All I remember is how badly I wanted to give them the same consideration they gave their child.

There are times in life or work when it will be difficult to stay disciplined, especially when a situation hits a button. I discovered how important it was to identify those buttons that have the ability set you off course and use them in training.

Prepare for them by running scenarios, even if it's just in your head. When faced with the real thing, professionalism and discipline will kick in. And if you realize that you need to rely on a team member, like I did in that situation, prepare.

Chapter 8

AVENUES OF APPROACH AND ESCAPE

#1 - Always know your avenues of approach.

Identify the best possible approach to put you in a position of advantage for the situation at hand.

#2 - Always know your avenues of escape.

Know the best possible ways to pull back, regroup, or extract once the objective has been met or achieved. In business, this may be called an exit strategy.

Notice that it says avenues, meaning *all* avenues. If you only identify and plan for one, you're destined to have a run in with Mr. Murphy.

REAL WORLD SWAT

Sometimes the best lessons are learned when the operation does not happen at all.

In the thousands of operations I've taken part in, I have never been as scared as the time I learned these lessons first-hand.

The scene was a *buy rip* taking place in a crowded business parking lot. (A buy rip is when drug dealers make an exchange of drugs for cash with an undercover cop or informant.) These operations are inherently dangerous but this case was far and above a normal situation because it involved a prominent gang in the area who were known to be drug and arms dealers. They actively looked for the opportunity to shoot at police officers and were rewarded by their organizations for doing so. Our intel was solid on this group of individuals and they would never go to a buy without four individuals in the vehicle—all of them armed. This was a very dangerous group and investigators had been working hard to break into this ring of drug and arms dealers for quite some time.

The opportunity came when this group finally agreed to do a buy with our undercover in a public parking lot within the next twenty-four hours. Our team was notified to respond to the investigations office where we were briefed. The lead investigator was a seasoned top-notch detective who I had worked with countless times over the past several years. When he was doing the brief, I noticed he was physically shaking, stuttering a bit, and there was very little color in his face. Something was different about this operation. This guy had been in some of the hairiest situations I could think of and had handled them just like another day at the office.

After the briefing, scout teams were sent out, operators were gearing up, sandboard diagrams were created, and assignments were made according to the intel that was coming back from the scout teams. Team leaders and members were focused on finding the best avenues of approach and escape, creating primary, contingency, and go-to-hell plans.

While all this was taking place, someone grabbed my arm. It was the lead investigator. He pulled me aside, looked me square in the eyes and said, "Hargraves, don't you let 'em get a shot off!" His face was white and I could see real concern in his demeanor.

To be frank, it was all pretty routine until then. Knowing this guy as well as I did and the fact that he didn't get shaken easily made me realize that there was a very good chance this op could go bad unless everything was executed perfectly. On a SWAT team, perfect execution is always the expectation and part of the way we achieved that was by taking the emotion out of the situation and executing flawlessly. This encounter with my friend did not help the situation.

It's hard to explain the feeling you get right before you knowingly enter into a life-or-death situation. Many operations don't become life or death until the threat appears and by then you don't have the time to sit around and think about it. Those are the easy ones, the ones we train for and only require trained surgical reaction. When you know it's a deadly situation and you have the time to process it, that's difficult.

It's also a time when your ability to learn is accelerated.

This would be an assault on a vehicle full of armed cop killers. Vehicle assaults are by nature some of the most difficult types of operations, but we trained for them frequently and it was the cards we were dealt at this time. Given the topography of the parking lot, we were limited on how we could approach this vehicle depending on where the buy rip would take place. We had to plan according to worst-case scenario, which frankly was the most likely scenario. Anything out of the ordinary would result in the subjects fleeing the scene and/or a possible gunfight.

The best choice was to have the team concealed in a van that was disguised as a phone company's vehicle. This would allow us the ability to close the open distance in the parking lot without raising too much concern. The perimeter was a mixture of cops disguised as civilians milling around, telephone repair workers, and strategically placed snipers.

The deliberate plan was to wait until the undercover made the drug buy, at which time he would communicate a specific word while talking to the dealers. That word keyed the raid, at which time our "phone van" would drive over to the perpetrators vehicle and pull sharply in front of them, with the sliding door facing the hood of their car. Simultaneously, another under cover vehicle would pull behind their car, boxing them in. The undercover would be making the buy at the passenger door and attempt to hold their attention until the van was in place. Then the doors would open, distraction devices would deploy, and in less than one second they would be greeted with an unexpected display of submachine guns at every angle.

My assignment was to be the first out of the sliding door, cross the hood of the perp's vehicle, and position on the front passenger door. One of the dangers of an assault like this lies in the positioning of your team around the vehicle. It creates a possible cross fire situation, which makes it extremely important that we execute our shots with surgical precision. My immediate assignment was to look for any active shooters while en route to my position and if encountered, neutralize that threat. Now, where these bandits were known to be armed during drug or arms deals, we had high chances of them attempting a shot.

We sat in the van for what seemed like forever going over our assignments and possible scenarios and solutions. The avenues of approach and escape were the primary focus of concern. Hours dragged on while anticipation and tension rose. Updates were given through our earpieces, with reports ranging from "The bad guys are changing the location," to "It's going down now, get ready!"

Finally, the perps car pulled into the parking lot with four subjects inside. Over the radio we heard the positioning and movements of the car and I could feel the anticipation nearing an end. I did one last press check on my MP5 and thought, "Thank heavens, let's get this done!" Just as our van began to move, the perps vehicle took off and left the parking lot.

I learned more about avenues of approach and escape during these painstaking hours of anticipation than I would have ever retained otherwise. There is something about being in that moment before the heat of battle that opens sensors in the brain to process at a very accelerated rate. It's pure uninterrupted focus. These moments are fueled by the fear of what could be a complete and total disaster. It's that same instinctive mindset we discussed earlier that creates this perfect opportunity to learn. Seize those moments of learning. Create them if you can.

BESWAT EXERCISE

Think about moments when you've had to act on pure instinct.

At the beginning of the book we talked about finding a hornet on you, and there are a lot of similar situations that will create the same scenario from walking into a spider web to leaning too far back in a chair. Those are physical responses to a survival instinct. The *No-Fail Mindset* is figuring out how to upgrade that reaction so it's occurring with every element of your life, from turning in a project at work to taking a snap in a football game. The stakes must be that high.

Take some time to jot down ways you can create those stakes with elements of your job or position.

Chapter 9

LEADERSHIP

On a SWAT team there is no MVP. The unit is supreme due to each operator being a vital component to the team and utilizing that team member's strengths. Missing one operator or having a weak operator lends a crack in the armor thereby making the unit susceptible to failure, which is not an option. The leader of the team is just one more essential member of the unit.

I don't want to diminish the value of leadership; a great leader alone can, and will, transform underperforming teams. But if you're looking to become a leader for accolades and attaboys, call your mother. They're not expected on SWAT and they don't belong on any team that needs to operate with a No-Fail Mindset.

Due to this need for cohesiveness, many decisions are brought to the team, discussed, implemented, and trained on. Great Leaders don't throw out orders they are not willing to fulfill on their own and in many occasions will be in the trenches operating beside their fellow operators conducting duties considered petty or difficult. Leaders find opportunities to be great teammates.

Great leaders don't pass the buck. They recognize their position and make the tough calls when needed. They also use the knowledge and skills of the operators around them to make those calls. The final decision might be yours as a leader, but you want the success to be the team's.

Part of being a great leader is also taking accountability for your decisions. It's not a two way street for leaders. If your decision elicits successful results, the teams wins. If your decision has unsuccessful results, that failure is on you as the leader. Operators must have the desire to follow their leaders. When the leader takes accountability for the team, it creates accountability at all levels. This creates a team that respects each other and will do anything for each other.

REAL WORLD SWAT

Remember the SWAT school? My Lieutenant literally broke his neck on day 7. If you knew this guy you would know there is no *give up* in his vocabulary. He was negotiating a drill where columns of PTMs (in full tac. kit) were passing other PTMs overhead. While he was the one overhead, there was an obvious disconnect with the two PTMs holding him at the end of the column. My Lieutenant was dropped and landed square on his neck. The instructors immediately saw he was injured and he was rushed to the hospital. After being treated, they diagnosed him with severe whiplash. Despite the agonizing pain, he immediately requested to return to his team and finish his training. Within about an hour he was back in the heat of it.

Battling through the immense pain, he made it through this incredibly demanding school and went on to graduate. The only way that was possible was because he refused to give up and let his teammates down. He knew something more was wrong with him but he pressed on, insisting that he finish the training. Really, I think he was telling himself there is no way he wanted to start the hell of SWAT school all over again!

On the drive home, he felt his throat swelling shut and called his wife who immediately told him to go to the nearest hospital. After several scans and review from the radiologists, they discovered his neck was broken. I'm sure he was thankful to complete the school after already enduring a week of the training, but looking back he's even luckier he didn't wind up paralyzed.

That's also how he led, every day. We knew we could count on him, regardless of what came at us. We knew that when the going got bad he wasn't going to quit on us.

SHIT DUTY

A day in the life of a full time SWAT operator does not always consist of the high-speed, low drag stuff you see in the movies! Hours upon hours are spent preparing for events that may never happen. *What if* scenarios become part of your regular thoughts. Daily routine and consistency become a thing of the past.

As another example of what lengths leaders need to go to, there's shit duty. In operations, things literally get Shipped High In Transit—resulting in S.H.I.T. duty for operators.

Every job has mundane tasks, it's how you flip your mindset that makes you SWAT.

REAL WORLD SWAT

When the pager goes off, many of the callouts are nothing shy of shit duty, and I mean that literally! For example, getting intel that drugs are being transported into the state prison via anal cavity of an inmate on a supervised work crew.

Sure, It all starts out okay with the long-range surveillance and securing video footage of the inmate sneaking out of the supervising officers field of view to a pre-designated drug drop. Watching the inmate swallow two small balloons of heroin and stuff an additional eight, one-inch diameter balloons up his rectum while thinking nobody can see him. (Ya, I know! The math doesn't seem to add up!)

Then, as he returns into the state prison, being there to pull him aside for a few questions. The value of 10 heroin balloons in a state prison? (At the time I wrote this, a *pinhead* of heroin was worth $60, so you can imagine what this amount was going for!). The look on the inmate's face when you show him the video? Priceless! The rectum balloons seem to come out easier than they went in. Unfortunately, those two balloons he swallowed need to come out as well. It's called Shit Duty. Sorta gives a whole new meaning to the acronym S.H.I.T.—Shipped High In Transit. The next 12-24 hours you and your partner are sitting in a dry cell with the inmate, a five gallon bucket, a see-through plastic bag and a can of Lysol! I'll let your imagination work that out.

My point is, there will always be parts of the job that are considered petty, undesirable, or a waste of your talent. These parts offer amazing opportunities for leaders to lead. Nobody wants to follow a professional delegator into a dogfight. If the team knows their leaders are willing to do what ever it takes to win, so will they. From the moment I was accepted into the Special Operations Unit, never was there an indication that I was not an absolute essential component of the team. This was known partly because we knew we were the best at what we did, otherwise we would not be there. But also because it was the culture of this team, that the leaders would show up willing and capable to do any task, despite their rank or the nature of the task.

Ultimately, your boss is generally not who you think it is. In SWAT it may be the victim you're protecting, their families, or the media—especially if something goes wrong. In business, your boss is the client you're working for. On an athletic team, it's the fans in the stands. These are your bosses and they ultimately have the power to fire you at any given time. Figure out who your true boss is and identify their pain points, manage those and integrate them into your **No-Fail Mindset**.

Chapter 10

ACCOUNTABILITY AND CONSEQUENCES

Certainly we could dig up a few examples in history where a SWAT team has failed. Disasters happen and I assure you, when they do, everything gets put under the microscope. Investigators, the public, the media, and most importantly, the teams themselves analyze and dissect the actions of that team and what went wrong.

It's interesting that when faced with life or death decisions, the SWAT operators must determine their course of action within milliseconds while everyone else has months or years to scrutinize over their actions to determine if they were correct. The good news is, with so much attention to each debacle—along with the ever-present risk of giving the ultimate sacrifice—tactical teams have been forced to create tactics that win at all costs.

The fact is, when something does go wrong, it's usually because one or more of the tactics and strategies used by these elite teams were overlooked.

Even though SWAT does have many people and higher-ups holding them accountable, during the operation they answer to their training and instinct, relying on their training in that moment. That's part of why their success is second to none. They answer to each other, they commit to saving the lives of the innocent, and they willingly put their lives on the line.

Doctors have similar scenarios. There are circumstances in emergency rooms and surgeries when a doctor has a millisecond to make a decision that might cost someone their life. After the procedure, everyone from the patient to the hospital board has a right to second-guess what the doctor didn't have time to think about. SWAT and other high-pressure jobs also have bosses, but in that moment they rely on training and instinct. As an operator, you rely on your disciplined training and moral compass. When your life or someone else's life is in imminent danger, you respond with like force. You don't have the luxury to worry about what the media is going to say, how the mayor is going to evaluate your actions, you act. You depend on your training and you act.

There are huge consequences to taking a life, to saving a life, to dying to save a life. The media and the community devise their own story and may or may not have all the facts, who weren't there, who didn't understand the consequences at stake when lives hung in the balance.

But we can't allow these factors to cloud our trained response in the moment of a critical decision. Neither can a doctor saving a life, and neither can you if you want to operate with a *No-Fail Mindset*.

BESWAT EXERCISE

What would you do if your every move was later scrutinized beneath a microscope? If tomorrow you started acting like it would be, would the way you work, train, and live change?

I implore you to be honest with yourself.

If you would approach your job or tasks differently, then you're not currently operating at the level that's required of a **No-Fail Mindset**.

Chapter 11

STRENGTHS VS. POLITICS

Seniority, favoritism, tenure and the political influence of preferential hiring regarding age, race, or gender have absolutely no place on a SWAT team. If I'm bold enough to say so, they have no place on *any* team and are one of the biggest—if not *the* biggest weaknesses of business-focused thinking.

Further, the lack of such ridiculous concepts contributes heavily to the success that tactical teams enjoy. This is a common cancer, killing the productivity in all types of businesses large and small, including our local, state, and federal government.

The finest tactical teams in the world are built around the strengths of their operators.

Consider the following scenario.

You have two operators; one is 6'5" and a senior operator to the other who stands at 5'10." Both operators posses relatively the same skill sets despite the additional experience of the senior operator. The mission they are about to enter is a dynamic entry into a hostile room. The question is, which operator should be assigned the prestigious position of point man and enter the room first?

A common response in traditional business today would be to give the operator who has seniority the point position, and in this scenario that could result in a deadly mistake! To put the taller operator on point because he has seniority and wants to be the first through the door could drastically hinder the team because his backup man can't see over the top of him. This type of rationale is not only ineffective, it gets people killed! Yet, it's truly amazing how many companies are operating with that type of mentality. Only the most qualified consistent operator in every sense of the term will fill a position! Your position on the team is a direct result of your strengths. Not your seniority or your relationships with key players. If someone comes along that is stronger than you at the position you hold, you will lose your position. This is a skill/result-based decision and is always challengeable. This creates and stimulates the need to be the best at what you do! There is no option to get comfortable in your position. If you make the decision to stop progressing, there is always the chance you will be replaced by someone better at your job and the best part is, the operators can only blame themselves.

Not only does this elicit team members to be the best at what they do but to actively find ways to become better than they already are. Identifying and utilizing the strengths of a team goes so much deeper than talent. As indicated in the previous example, certain assignments may be a result of the size, gender, personality or race of the operator. In this line of work, results are not measured in what's politically correct, but in life or death.

Ask yourself this question, if the assignment your taking on could result in life or death, would you choose to have the same people around you? Further, would you choose yourself for the job you are taking on? If there is any hesitation in your answer, that is a good indication of weakness.

Business can be cutthroat, political, and self-serving. Many corporate structures are even set up to promote individualism and then wonder why their teams aren't meeting goals or don't work well together. There is absolutely no room for playing favorites.

The team is only as strong as the weakest link!

REAL WORLD SWAT

As a new operator on a SWAT team, it's hard to explain how you feel during the staging period before a high-risk operation is executed. It almost seemed the easy operations were the ones that just happened, immediate response with no time to think. The longer that staging time period is, the more intense it gets.

As more time goes by, you're able to put more thought into it, thereby creating more anticipation. Most of this time is spent running through the details of your assignment and the deliberate action plan—running *what if* scenarios in your head, going over the intel, anticipating what the bad guys are going to do, running more *what if* scenarios. By the time you get the order to execute, it feels like your blood is going to bust through your skin. This is good!

One call came in from our investigative unit reporting a state parolee was running a drug lab out in the sticks of rural Utah. Quite a bit of intel had been collected on this operation so the briefing was well informed.

Our scout teams went out and returned leaving snipers with eyes on the target. The scouts reported back that the major issue was the avenue of approach. The target home was on top of a slight hill with acres of open land surrounding it. There was almost no cover or concealment for the team as we approached the target.

According to the informant, the parolee had several firearms in the house, including long-range rifles. To prevent the team from being exposed for such a long approach, we decided to find an old farm truck and use it as the approach vehicle. We found a big, old, hay-hauling truck that was perfect. It concealed the entry team in the back and fit right into the environment. This truck gave us the ability to get right to the front of the house without being detected.

It's normal that we layout the structure and interior of the house in a big parking lot or field to practice our entry. We call this sandboarding. This process creates a mental picture and helps with the flow once you get into the actual space. As we wrapped up our deliberate action plan, we received a report over the radio that one of our main subjects had just left the residence. Not wanting to compromise the operation, we had to wait for the subject to return. Minutes turned into hours and I remember waking up with my headphones in my ears propped up against a wall.

I sat there looking at all the junior operators pacing back and forth working through their assignments, asking questions and gathering information that would assist them. Almost immediately, one of the newbies came over to me and made a comment like, "Man how do you stay so calm?" It was that moment when I realized I had allowed myself to become desensitized and slipped into a dangerous level of comfort. I welcomed the wake up call and used it to snap me out of it.

There is a distinct difference in being able to stay calm, cool and collected, and becoming complacent. Many people confuse complacency for competency. It's easy to do, especially if your talking about an icon in your industry that has a highly decorated past. With this type of selection process, those who choose to stop advancing and rest on the laurels of their past, will quickly be replaced.

It's not what you've done, its what you're doing now that justifies your position and separates the elite from the standard.

Chapter 12

TEAMWORK

The team. A group of people linked in common purpose to achieve super-human results.

Make no mistake; teams can be volatile without proper training and structure. Being oversized, undersized, or having too many working parts can be a hindrance. However, a properly constructed team offers the ability to accomplish things no single person can.

Selection

The selection process is as important to teamwork as getting the individuals to work together as a team. By discovering and identifying the gaps in a team and making selections based on the strengths needed to fill those gaps is essential. Having the wrong people on a team or the wrong leadership can prove to be worse than going it alone.

Commitment/Purpose/Pride

Teams work because individuals make a purposeful commitment to each other and have pride in their combined purpose.

I don't care what your job is, what you think of it, or what you'd prefer to be doing, you are where you are right now, what's the point in showing up half ass? You must have commitment, purpose and pride in what you do, but even more important, each member of the team must be ALL IN!

Individuals by nature become demanding. The only thing the team demands is the all-in commitment of the of the individual!

Every team needs that one good firefight

It's an amazing feeling when you know those surrounding you are as committed to your success as they are their own because it's one and the same. Their failures becomes yours, your success is theirs. Pure investment in the greater purpose. The immersion in a hostile environment has a way of bringing that out in teams.

A close friend and great operator currently serving with the elite U.S. Delta Force teams said to me, "Every great team needs that one good firefight". There is so much to be taken from those words. Whether it's a massive business project, a jury trial, or combat, going through the heat of it with your team not only unifies the team, but can also expose areas that need work.

The Blue Code

On the topic of teamwork, let's address a point that is undoubtedly a sore spot for many who haven't been in a special operations environment.

Most people have heard about a situation where an officer allows another officer to slide after they're pulled over for speeding or another infraction. This makes non-officers and civilians angry because they weren't offered the same courtesy and probably got a speeding ticket. Many call this the *Blue Code* and I hope to shed some light in a way you can not only understand the *Blue Code* as a tool (when used properly), but also recognize its importance, and see how you already apply the same code in your own life.

Now, first, not all cops honor the *Blue Code* and it doesn't happen all the time, but I will go as far to say that almost every operator on a tactical team will honor this code. So when it does happen, why? Why do operators honor the *Blue Code* and cover for each other when they screw up?

It goes back to the consequence of a teammate's death. We take that very seriously and can't turn it off. When we walk into a situation, we've committed to covering each other, and I know that my team has my six. I can always handle what's in front of me, but to do that, I have to know that someone else is handling what's behind me.

The Blue Code goes beyond covering for and "helping" a fellow operator. When used properly, the code holds a specific importance, one you can apply in your personal life.

Consider immersing yourself in an environment where your craft is to protect and serve others that you don't even know, from evils nobody wants anything to do with. Further, you know it is not a task that you can accomplish alone, and in order to survive, you must depend on others. Then, day after day, you willfully throw yourself into these situations in the interest of humanity to provide at least some equalizing impact for the greater good. If that isn't enough, add on the fact that you spend more than twice the amount of time with these individuals than you do your own family. A relationship, built on common purpose, soaked in trust and seared with the blood of your life. At no time is there ever a question whether or not you would die for the one next to you, It's a given. Then it becomes your purpose, the reason you excel at your craft, to protect the ones next to you because somehow, there lives mean more than your own. This defines the relationship between operators. If it doesn't, you're probably not the right person for the job and I certainly wouldn't want you covering my six.

Now, if you're a parent, I'm guessing most of you get it when put into that context. We all honor the *Blue Code* throughout our lives. We take care of our loved ones. For many readers, these types of relationships are even built without the circumstances described above or from blood relation. It may be an assumption, but I believe everyone reading this has that type of a relationship with someone in his or her life. Civilians have been known to break the law for their loved ones and are willing to pay those penalties.

I'm not suggesting that you do this, but merely trying to illustrate the point to better understand why officers may be willing to forgive each other for breaking the speed limit or other minor infractions. There are lines and consequences where that kind of forgiveness would be unacceptable.

So ask yourself, if it were that person in your life who made a mistake and it were you that had the power to assist them in some way, to what extent would you go to protect them? If you caught them speeding, would you let it slide, or would you dial 911 from the passenger seat and report them?

As operators, we are held to the standard of law-abiding citizens, maybe even to a higher standard than the average citizen. Does this mean we don't make mistakes? No. Show me a cop, or anyone for that matter, who claims to be perfect and I'll show you a poser full of hypocrisy. Having said that, there is a distinct line that comes with *the shield*. People make mistakes and mistakes can be corrected. It's when the intent lies on the other side of what you're attempting to uphold that makes you unworthy of the code. In other words, willfully participating as a criminal under the guise of a position honored to protect and serve with intent to harm or take another's agency.

Save these *dirty cops* with bad intent, my experience is that most operators will do whatever is in their power to take care of another operator when they screw up. It's an instinctive, protective nature that one can't help, and no, it's not necessarily right or fair. But I can tell you, these small acts of camaraderie don't go unnoticed and can be a powerful tool between personnel and even agencies that don't work together on a regular basis. If the men and women in uniform are doing their best to uphold the oath taken, the mishaps are few and minor, most often accompanied in a moment of poor choice and corrected quickly.

Chapter 13

POSITIONING AND FLOW

Teams become invincible when the positions, skills, and coverage can overlap. In addition to positioning operators strategically for maximum success, people can, and will, constantly cover for each other. When a team is built on the strengths of the operators, you find yourself with a highly effective unit. But this team must also have the ability to keep moving despite the obstacles encountered and accomplish the mission. Cross-training yourself to become operational on the positions around you becomes essential. We call this flow.

In business, this can also prevent individuals from hoarding information or becoming a liability because if they were removed from the situation no one would be able to cover for them, which has the potential to put teams, projects, and even entire businesses at risk.

On SWAT, when a team goes through a building, the operators have the ability to constantly rotate, flowing over one another, with each operator taking up a new position as they set again. The team flows through the building like water through a maze.

As you review the positioning and components of a 5-man SWAT entry team, compare them to your own team or project to discover ways to use these tactics.

360 Degree Coverage

This coverage is used in SWAT teams to provide coverage from all angles of attack and prevent vulnerability. SWAT teams rely on their members to cover their blind spots. Each member's parameters overlap, ensuring double coverage for added protection.

There will be times at the point of execution where an operator may become distracted or focused on a specific area or component. This calls for that operator's teammates to fill in the gaps and cover that operator's area of assignment that is left exposed. We call this having each other's six, which is literally that area behind you, the area you cannot see and where you are most vulnerable.

Knowing that your team or coworkers will intercept anything you don't see coming creates an enormous amount of unity in purpose and mutual respect within the team.

Part of the team-building process is not only practicing this principle in training and execution but also living it in all aspects of the relationship between team members. It was common practice on our team to constantly remind each other that we've got their six.

Specialty Assignments

Successful teams identify the strengths needed to achieve 360-degree coverage and assign specialists to those positions creating a dream team of operators. So what happens in the event an operator is distracted, sick or otherwise unable to do their job? On a SWAT team, each member of a specific unit is cross-trained on each position. Though it may not be your particular specialty, you are well-versed in the position and able to step in at anytime.

For example, the operators of a 5-man entry team (called a stick) will have the following assignments but each operator is trained on each position and will crossover when needed without hesitation to ensure flow.

Point

The first operator in. Point handles the immediate threat, sets the pace, and identifies obstacles and threats.

BUM (BackUp Man)

The second operator in. BUM covers the point's six, and handles the next threat or assists in the primary threat.

Trailer

The third operator in. Trailer reads and reacts to the BUM, cleans up and covers additional blind zones, and assists in additional threats.

Team Leader

Typically takes position of trailer in the stick (leading from trenches), handles all the communication, both with control and verbally directing the team.

Breacher

Blows the door and will precede or follow the Medic. This operator overcomes obstacles hard or soft with whatever means necessary to insure the flow of the team and its mission. When not breaching, this operator will fit into the stick as Point, BUM, or Trailer.

Medic

Due to the nature of the assignment, each team is equipped with a Medic. First responsible for the team members in the event of injury then to others needing attention. If none is needed, Medic will fit into the stick as a Point, BUM or Trailer.

However your team is structured, this ability to crossover in position is an essential part of creating successful teams that flow and can overcome any objective they face. (These are very brief setups and descriptions of the positions. In the **BeSWAT** advanced workshops, we identify how each **BeSWAT Tactic** applies specifically to your objective.)

Chapter 14

EXECUTION

Would you accept 99.9% efficiency in your operation? Think about it, that is a mere 1/10 of 1% defect!

Most people not only think that would be acceptable, but would see a dramatic improvement in their results. However, consider these statistics[1] using a 99.9% efficiency:

18 planes would crash every day.

10 newborns would be dropped every day.

24.8 million dollars would be erroneously transferred into accounts daily.

3,700 prescriptions would be filled incorrectly every day.

500 incorrect surgical procedures would be done this week.

That isn't good enough for SWAT. The expectation is perfect surgical results. By following the rule of percentages and ensuring preparation to execution is 99:1, when everything is on the line

---

1 Data gathered on or around May 2000

the execution will feel as easy and natural as breathing. This is where all of that preparation and training pays off.

There is one other advantage of the *No-Fail Mindset* and this applies to everyone, not just SWAT. We go into every situation already knowing what the threshold is and what lengths we're going to go to, especially if the unexpected happens. Your competition might not have (in most cases, they haven't). This gives you a serious advantage and you're going to catch them off guard because they haven't thought through the stakes.

In SWAT, we are committed before we even arrive. We have already made the tough decisions and are willing to give our lives if necessary. We've trained with 99:1 and perform snap to snap every time. This gives us a massive advantage. The bad guys, on the other hand, don't even *know* we are coming, and when they find out, they still have to make those serious choices. Are they willing to die for their cause? Do they have a plan? Have they trained to create surgical precise response? Are they going to let up when it gets tough?

SWAT dictates the pace because we've set the course of action and the bad guys have to respond how we want them responding. We go in with speed, surprise, and violence of action with our *No-Fail Mindset* fully engaged. All of the sudden, the bad guys have to figure out what they want to do and what's the level of their commitment, all while chaos is raining down on them; they get caught by surprise.

Speed, Surprise, and Violence of Action

This is the unsung code of a SWAT operator. Preferably all three components should be in place at the time of execution to insure an operation will go smoothly. Minimum two of these components need to be present to engage in the operation.

Speed

Many people mistake this for going fast. Smooth and surgical is fast. Its important to remember you can only move as fast as you can effectively operate! Choppy, non-fluid movements and moving faster than you can effectively operate will cause mistakes and a ripple effect behind you. These mistakes must be corrected, which takes time, which slows the entire process down. Proper flow is also achieved by being timely, accurate, reading the operators to either side of you, and ensuring 360 degrees of coverage.

Surprise

Do not let the opposition see you coming! This element lets you control the environment. Whether it is your timing, proposal, technology, or game plan, keep your cards close. By the time the opposition sees what you are doing they don't have the time to react. Or in the case of a presentation to a client, they don't have the ability to come into the meeting with a prejudice or pre-conceived notions.

Violence of Action

When you go to work, make your work product hit with such overwhelming force and focus that it completely stuns your opposition. Be in a constant state of learning evaluating and progressing.

BESWAT TACTIC

T-Shot

A distraction technique used to achieve a goal. Using one *motor-mouth* to retain attention while two other operators position themselves optimally to achieve the goal.

What's the T-Shot in sports, or your business? It can be a diversion your opponent or competitor didn't see coming so you can get into position. There are several ways to use a T-Shot creatively and effectively.

Chapter 15

CONCLUSION

After a traumatic experience, it's common to hear the people involved say that they felt like time slowed down. I researched this phenomenon to help me try and understand what happens and while there's no science that proves time slows down, there is an explanation that I found fascinating and wanted to analyze.

Our brains are constantly taking in vast amounts of information—every detail about what's taking place in the world around us, from colors, to how fast cars are moving past, to faces, to temperature, to perceived threats while we're standing in the grocery aisle. These details are carryovers from our caveman days when everything *was* a threat. In most countries, we can safely proceed through our day without needing this barrage of information, so our brains discard the details as junk and time moves at a regular pace.

But, when you're in a life-or-death situation, you're aware of every single piece of information you're taking in because you're now in ultimate survival mode. Those perceived threats have become reality. In this moment, your brain needs you paying attention to every single detail to keep you alive.

For more clarification, I sat down with a neuroscientist and this was his additional input:

There are places in our brains that process specific information like the senses and muscle movements.
Most of the rest of the brain is divided into two networks.
One is called the default mode network, which processes

our thoughts, ideas, and sensations from within our bodies.

The other network is called the attention control network and pays attention to the outside world. This network registers what happens around us, where it's happening, and processes novelty detection.

These two networks are opposed and we see this directly with brain imaging. When one is active, the other shuts down. That is why when you are paying close attention to the outside world, the voice in your head shuts off. When you are lost in thought, you are oblivious to the outside world—At least in healthy brains. When these networks don't function independently, you have distractibility and poor concentration. Most mental illness includes these two networks not functioning independently enough.

When you are paying careful attention to your senses, you later perceive this time between thoughts as though time has slowed down. –Jeffrey Anderson, M.D., Ph.D.

Whichever explanation, we see that you could never operate at that hyper-attention level to the outside world on a constant basis and still be able to function very well in normal daily life. This is one reason why the 99:1 parts preparation to execution is important. Being *really* prepared for what you're going to do makes the execution easier because you've created a habit of operating at perfection.

Back to the trauma and time slowing down, if you've been involved in a car accident, you didn't have to think about how to drive the car to do everything possible to avoid the accident and get to safety. Your mechanics reacted in a precise surgical manner and you knew which way to turn the wheel and which pedals to push. And the longer you've been driving (preparing) the higher the chances of avoiding an accident altogether when something goes wrong (execution.) It's the same in life, in your career, on the field, we just don't believe we're capable of slowing down time and operating at that level in non life threatening events like designing a presentation or meeting with a new client.

There is a way to flip that on, even if only for moments throughout the day, without a life-or-death danger present.

You just have to identify it, and train yourself to use it.

I created this book to share what works, but it all hinges on the *No-Fail Mindset*.

While SWAT has a unique way of naturally flipping this switch in operators, it's certainly not unique to SWAT. I've seen it work in nearly every profession.

What we have talked about today isn't a theory. These tactics have been created and implemented on tactical teams not only because they work, but because they save lives. Now that you have this information, not putting it into action would be like having a special uniform you can wear that will ensure victory, but not using it until you get to the championship, which doesn't make any sense because if you wait until the championship, you'll never get there.

When it's time to execute, the *No-Fail Mindset* is a mentality that must be carried snap to snap, task to task, moment to moment. All to often I hear that some tasks are just too large to approach with this kind of intensity. Yes large complex tasks can seem overwhelming when viewed as a whole and this is where most fail because it's so large and impossible when viewed that way. But those big tasks become manageable when you attack them snap to snap. Honestly, that was the only way to survive SWAT school. You couldn't focus on the end because it was too daunting and overwhelming. I had to go snap to snap, I could say, "I'm going to run to the next hill top, and now the next sign, and now the next wall." After a while, I'd piled up enough little steps and looked back at what initially seemed impossible. Big projects are the same. What's the next step that can be done this week, or today, or this hour? Some tasks do take longer, but the **BeSWAT** tactics can still be applied in manageable segments day after day after day.

I've included techniques and tactics in here that have given SWAT teams unfounded success. By implementing the same *No-Fail Mindset*, you can take your actions to the next level and **BeSWAT**.

I'm not going to tell you that being SWAT in everything you do is going to be easy, but I will tell you that it works! I'm also not going to tell you that you'll be guaranteed a win every time, sometimes the guy on the other side of the ball will be hungrier and will want it more—he'll be the Will Smith of an opponent and he'll never quit until he dies. You have to decide to want it more than anyone else. Couple that with BeSWAT and you *will* be unstoppable.

Mindset is everything. Mindset is the key.

Truly, the secret ingredient is being able to show up and flip the switch. There were other great tactics, techniques and strategies in here, but none of it will happen if you can't flip into your *No-Fail Mindset*.

Flipping the switch is different for everyone. We all have our own motivators and personal situations that are as unique as we are. But I have seen ordinary people discover this secret and become masterful at what they do. I believe that every single person has the capability to be remarkable, given the opportunity and discovery of this mindset.

I saw myself as an ordinary guy. The reason I figured out the *No-Fail Mindset* was because my life was on the line and I saw what seemed like average people turn into amazing operators simply because of their natural instincts. Without that threat of life or death, they may not have been part of something that great.

Before this discovery, I believed that greatness was reserved for certain people with certain privilege. But that concept was completely destroyed by the accomplishments of a team—my team—comprised of seemingly average, everyday guys. Only then did I make the connection to the elite of the elite. They had the same traits, they were using the same SWAT *No-Fail mindset*, they just didn't know it.

You have the capability to create something phenomenal and life-altering if that's your desire.

Whether you think you're extraordinary or not, you are.

You are as great as your mentors and heroes, the only thing that separates you from them is your decision to apply your *No-Fail Mindset*.

In summary, the other key components to BeSWAT are:

Identify the strengths of competent individuals.

Link them in common purpose.

Arm them with special weapons and tactics.

Treat it like it's a life or death situation with the *No-Fail Mindset*.

Master your craft with 99% Preparation and 1% Execution.

Be invested in a team that is built on the strengths of each team member.

Have commitment, purpose, and pride in your team. Always have each other's 6!

Execute to perfection with speed, surprise, and violence of action.

There is no question that if you take every snap, every decision, every project with a *No-Fail Mindset* and implement these tactics, you'll find yourself and your team overwhelming your competition!

Thanks

This book has been a taste of what **BeSWAT** and the *No-Fail Mindset* can create in your life. Implement them, and you'll see phenomenal results.

I also give more in-depth talks and seminars that can take you, your team, and your business to the next level.

Contact me for details.

801-330-6715

mike@beswat.com

http://beswat.com

I offer different levels of programming to meet your specific need and I've designed them to work independently of me so you learn the skills to flip your own switch today and every day thereafter.

Introductory Level

A Keynote presentation covering the topics and strategies addressed in the book, including an in-depth

look at the *No-Fail Mindset* and how your teams, players, and employees can benefit and implement them.

Mastery Level

A Keynote presentation, plus interactive scenarios and high-level training, customized to fit the time commitment you'd like to initiate for your operation. My team and I will assess your personnel and goals, creating BeSWAT situations to guide your success. By implementing the tools at this level, your team and business will be a weapon.

SWAT Camp

If you really want to take it to the next level, I offer SWAT Camp.

SWAT Camp is a 3-day training *as a SWAT team*. This immersive experience is unlike any training you've ever attended. We use hostages and weapons in simulations with debriefs and real-world experience. In less than three days I will identify everything from who your leaders are to where your weaknesses lie. This intensive training highlights the value of each team member. There is no hiding who you really are when the stakes are turned up like they are in SWAT Camp.

Thank you for taking the time to read **BeSWAT**. I wish you the best in your endeavors and in life.
—Mike

ABOUT THE AUTHOR

Michael Hargraves is recognized as an acclaimed keynote speaker, author, team-building trainer, and success coach. Mike's unique method of using SWAT tactics to achieve success is absolutely engaging and effective. What you walk away with is a mental strategy that will completely overwhelm the competition.

A dedicated husband and father of two, Mike has spent the last 15 years building, operating, and owning several successful businesses. Seeing the results of applying these tactics to his own businesses, he began consulting individuals and large companies alike increasing their productivity and profitability.

Mike has trained corporate teams, athletic teams, Leadership groups and SWAT teams to develop their skills, enhance teamwork and synergy to achieve extraordinary results.

Mike has delivered keynote speeches and strategy sessions to tens of thousands across the world including the United States, United Kingdom, New Zealand, Australia, Malaysia, and Canada.

Made in the USA
San Bernardino, CA
23 June 2020